Parable and Paradox

MALCOLM GUITE is Chaplain of Girton College, Cambridge. A performance poet and singer-songwriter, he lectures widely on poetry and theology in Britain and in North America. His poetry and faith blog: www.malcolmguite.wordpress.com receives many thousands of visits every week.

His previous poetry collections include **Sounding the Seasons** and **The Singing Bowl,** and he is the author of **Waiting on the Word: A poem a day for Advent, Christmas and Epiphany; Word in the Wilderness: a poem a day for Lent and Easter** and **Faith, Hope and Poetry.**

Parable and Paradox

Malcolm Guite

CANTERBURY
PRESS
Norwich

© Malcolm Guite 2016

First published in 2016 by the Canterbury Press Norwich
Editorial office
3rd Floor, Invicta House,
108–114 Golden Lane,
London EC1Y 0TG, UK

Canterbury Press is an imprint of Hymns Ancient & Modern Ltd
(a registered charity)
13A Hellesdon Park Road, Norwich,
Norfolk NR6 5DR, UK.

www.canterburypress.co.uk

British Library Cataloguing in Publication data

A catalogue record for this book is available
from the British Library

978 1 84825 859 4

Typeset by Regent Typesetting
Printed and bound in Great Britain by
CPI Group (UK) Ltd, Croydon

Contents

Parable and Paradox: 50 Sonnets on the Sayings of Jesus 28

For Richard Hays

Preface and Acknowledgements

This book takes its title from the sequence of 50 sonnets reflecting on the sayings of Jesus that forms its core. All poetry, however, avails itself of the wider symbolic reach of everyday experience which is the basis of any parable, and poetry is especially fitted to point towards and deepen that experience of paradox which pierces us so often when we try to grasp a spiritual truth. I hope therefore that *Parable and Paradox* can serve as an overall title for all the poems in this collection. The title sequence is intended as a companion and complement to the 70 sonnets on the Christian year contained in my book *Sounding the Seasons*. Whereas that sonnet sequence was rooted in the cycle of the year and dealt with faith thematically and topically, while also naturally drawing on Scripture, these new sonnets grew out of meditation on particular verses of Scripture, resting in and wrestling with the words the Gospels ascribe to the Word himself. Like the earlier sequence, these sonnets have been composed both for personal reading and for use in liturgy and prayer. To help with the latter I have provided an index of biblical passages to which the poems refer or on which they reflect.

They were composed over the course of a year in which I tried to respond, as honestly as I could, to lectionary readings as I heard them in church. In particular I wanted to get to grips with what might be called the 'hard sayings' of Jesus, the ones preachers sometimes prefer to avoid: 'sell all you have'; 'I have not come to bring peace but a sword', 'get thee behind me, Satan'. But I have also written about those sayings that kindle our hearts immediately and draw us deeper into the mystery of the kingdom: the beatitudes, the parables of the sower, the mustard seed, and the leaven. Contained within this longer sequence are several small sequences gathering together

xi

sayings that are themselves all linked. There is a sequence on the seven 'I AM' sayings in John's Gospel, a sequence of seven sonnets on the Lord's Prayer, and five sonnets on the Two Great Commandments. When it comes to hearing the words of Jesus, our great problem is overfamiliarity – we think we already know them; they are covered in what Coleridge called a 'film of familiarity'. It has been my aim in these poems to peel back that film, to be exposed again to the sayings in their new-ness and challenge, and to be as honest as I can in my response.

The whole experience of writing these poems has brought me back, time and again, to the centrality of Christ: not only of his teaching, but of his very person and being. I have become more and more aware of how everything coheres, connects, and is fulfilled in him: not simply the pages of the Old and New Testaments, but everything, from the smallest seed to the most distant star. This renewed understanding has shaped the choice and composition of the other poems in this collection and I hope the reader will be able to trace the threads of connec-tion that became apparent to me in composing and arranging these poems. Given this underlying sense of coherence in and through the sheer grace of Christ, it seemed fitting to finish the collection with a sort of thanksgiving and doxology, and 'Seven Whole Days', the little pendant sequence of roundels giving praise for and on each of the days of creation, is included to serve that purpose.

This collection was begun while I was artist in residence in the Divinity School at Duke University in North Carolina, and I am especially grateful to the Dean, Richard Hays, to whom this book is dedicated, for arranging that time for me and for the use of his office while I was there. Most of all, though, I valued the beautiful insights of his work on the New Testament, and especially on how it rereads and fulfils the Old, work that has deeply informed my own thinking. I continued my work on this book while spending time as a visiting fellow at St John's Col-lege, Durham and I am grateful to all those who made me so welcome there, as I am to Girton, my own college, for granting me the term's sabbatical in which I made these visits.

No poet works in isolation, however solitary they may be during the brief moments when they are physically writing. In her excellent books *The Company They Keep* and *Bandersnatch*, Diana Glyer has reminded me of what it is to be a writer in community, and I am very conscious of the networks, communities and individuals who have sustained my endeavours, encouraged my muse, and kindled my imagination. In particular, Michael Ward's editorial comments and insights into selection and sequencing were crucial to the making of this book. Three outstanding musicians and composers have been essential to the development of what I do here: Steve Bell, who asked me to write several of these poems for his *Pilgrim Year* project; J. A. C. Redford, who commissioned me to write the 'Ode to St Cecilia' and whose settings of my sonnets have been so inspiring; and Alana Levandoski, who commissioned me to write the meditation on Colossians with which this book opens. She set that poem in her beautiful album *Behold I Make All Things New*.

Also commissioned by Steve Bell, but written during the time I spent as a priest with Kate Gross, the sonnet 'Pilgrimage' was inspired by my conversations with Kate, and it was read, at her request, at both her baptism and her funeral. Kate was an inspiration to many and will live on through her brilliant book *Late Fragments*. 'Nicholas Ferrar' is dedicated to the memory of another remarkable woman, Susan Gray, who loved Little Gidding and whose last words to me when I gave her communion were 'In my end is my beginning'. The poems I have dedicated to Scott Cairns and Luci Shaw are testimony to the influence of their poetry and the example they have set me of faithfulness at once to the work and to the Word behind all works.

I have also been privileged to work with a number of visual artists who have responded to my work and in turn stimulated me to new writing. Faye Hall has made a number of paintings inspired by my poetry, which have in their turn re-inspired me. Some of these are now published in her book *Art Begets Art*. Stephanie Gehring has made beautiful calligraphic art from some of the poems I wrote while artist in residence at Duke, which are now on permanent exhibition there. I am grateful to two excellent photographers, Lancia Smith and Margot Krebs Neale, whose photographic images and collages in response to my poems draw out many new facets from my words. These can be found accompanying the poems on my Wordpress blog. The sequence 'In the Wilderness' in this book was a response to sketches sent to me by Adam Boulter for a sequence he was working on commissioned by Westminster Abbey, and the sonnets and finished paintings were exhibited together in St Margaret's Westminster in Lent 2015. The cover of this book is a detail from one of those paintings, *Jacob Wrestling with the Angel*. It portrays Jacob's encounter with the unknown Other as something between a wrestle and a dance, which seems to me to reflect something of my own dance and wrestle with the teachings of Jesus as I wrote this book.

In this, as in my other books for Canterbury Press, I have been encouraged by the support and enthusiasm of my editor Christine Smith.

Some of these poems have appeared elsewhere in journals or on music CDs, including *Theology*, *The Yale ISM Review*, *The St John's College Record*, and Steve Bell's album *Pilgrimage*. 'St Patrick' was first published in my Lent anthology *The Word in the Wilderness*, and 'Launde Abbey on St Lucy's Day' first appeared in my Advent anthology *Waiting on the Word*.

I have been greatly helped in my work as a poet by Philippa Pearson and Judith Tonry, acting respectively as PA and amanuensis, who have lifted from my shoulders burdens of work that would otherwise have crushed the muse.

Finally, I am grateful to Maggie, my wife, for her constant support, and for heroically managing the household during those times when I have been away as artist in residence, or on the road as a poet.

Everything Holds Together

Colossians 1.15–17: He is the image of the invisible God, the first-born of all creation; for in him all things in heaven and on earth were created, things visible and invisible, whether thrones or dominions or rulers or powers – all things have been created through him and for him. He himself is before all things, and in him all things hold together.

Everything holds together, everything,
From stars that pierce the dark like living sparks,
To secret seeds that open every spring,
From spanning galaxies to spinning quarks,
Everything holds together and coheres,
Unfolding from the centre whence it came.
And now that hidden heart of things appears,
The firstborn of creation takes a name.

And shall I see the one through whom I am?
Shall I behold the one for whom I'm made,
The light in light, the flame within the flame,
Eikon tou theou, image of my God?
He comes, a little child, to bless my sight,
That I might come to him for life and light.

For Scott Cairns

For everything coheres within the *Logos*;
Even those afternoons, lost in a maze,
A stupefaction in the face of *Chronos*,
When only Idiot Psalms can voice his praise.
Everything coheres; our unbelief
Makes up the score that underscores our faith.
Your poetry makes music of our brief
Epiphanies vouchsafed in love and wrath.

The man who harrowed hell gave you a map
That you might make for us a pilgrims' guide;
A mess of desolation laced with hope,
Communion with a whisky in the side.
As you restore the broken themes of praise
I lift my glass and bless our borrowed days.

Pilgrimage

In memoriam Kate Gross

Come dip a scallop shell into the font
For birth and blessings as a child of God.
The living water rises from that fount
Whence all things come, that you may bathe and wade
And find the flow, and learn at last to follow
The course of Love upstream towards your home.
The day is done and all the fields lie fallow,
One thing is needful, one voice calls your name.

Take the true compass now, be compassed round
By clouds of witness, chords of love unbound.
Turn to the Son, begin your pilgrimage,
Take time with him to find your true direction.
He travels with you through this darkened age
And wakes you every day to resurrection.

Ode to St Cecilia

You rested briefly here, Cecilia,
In this good ground, the Roman catacomb.
Its rounded vaults are rich with sudden sound
As pilgrims hymn you through the darkened air.
For you made music in your martyrdom,
Transposed the passion of your wedding night
To angel-given garlands, wreathed in light.
In all your three days dying you made room
For beautiful abundance, gifts and giving,
Your death was blessing and your passing praise,
As you gave way to grace,
Like music that still lives within its dying
And gives in giving place.

Cecilia, give way to grace again,
Transmute it into music for us all;
Music to stir and call the sleeping soul,
And set a counterpoint to all our pain,
To bless our senses in their very essence
And undergird our sorrow in good ground.
Music to summon undeserved abundance,
Unlooked-for over-brimming, rich and strong;
The unexpected plenitude of sound
Becoming song.

The Baton

Tap of a baton and the music starts,
Con brio and *Vivace*, full of life.
With a percussive hush and rush the strings,
Plucked on their pizzicato tenterhooks,
Begin a playful pulse that pulls you in,
Brimming with memories of spring and rhythm;
Of patterns patted out on your five fingers,
Delicious incantations, nursery rhymes,
The ways the farmer and the beggar ride,
Enchanted jiggle-juggle, swoop and swing.

You heard the baton tap before your birth,
Deep in the wombing dark, a pulsing beat;
The spring and source and rhythm of your life.
You heard the sound that measures all your years,
Your mother's heartbeat as it quickened yours,
Music before you had the ears to hear.

Now music is remaking memory
In repetitions, forward references,
The to and fro of making all things new,
Till tempo over-flows the temporary,
The beaten bars of time turn on their sides
And lift a ladder to the timeless realm.
You climb it into freedom till you reach
The limit and the centre of the dance:
Rich silence, as the baton comes to rest.

Smoke Rings from My Pipe

All the long day's weariness is done,
I'm free at last to do just as I will,
Take out my pipe, admire the setting sun,
Practise the art of simply sitting still.
Thank God I have this briar bowl to fill,
I leave the world with all its hopeless hype,
Its pressures, and its ever-ringing till,
And let it go in smoke rings from my pipe.

The hustle and the bustle, these I shun,
The tasks that trouble and the cares that kill,
The false idea that there's a race to run,
The pushing of that weary stone uphill,
The wretched iPhone's all-insistent trill,
Whingers and whiners, each with their own gripe,
I pack them in tobacco leaves until
They're blown away in smoke rings from my pipe.

And then at last my real work is begun:
My chance to chant, to exercise the skill
Of summoning the muses, one by one,
To meet me in their temple, touch my quill
(I have a pen but quills are better still),
And when the soul is full, the time is ripe,
Kindle the fire of poetry that will
Breathe and expand like smoke rings from my pipe.

Envoi
Prince, I have done with grinding at the mill,
These petty-pelting tyrants aren't my type,
So lift me up and set me on a hill,
A free man blowing smoke rings from his pipe.

And is it Not Enough?

And is it not enough that every year
A richly laden autumn should unfold
And shimmer into being leaf by leaf,
Its scattered ochres mirrored everywhere
In hints and glints of hidden red and gold
Threaded like memory through loss and grief,

When dusk descends, when branches are unveiled,
When roots reach deeper than our minds can feel
And ready us for winter with strange calm,
That I should see the inner tree revealed
And know its beauty as the bright leaves fall
And feel its truth within me as I am?

And is it not enough that I should walk
Through low November mist along the bank,
When scents of woodsmoke summon, in some long
And melancholy undertone, the talk
Of those old poets from whose works I drank
The heady wine of an autumnal song?

It is not yet enough. So I must try,
In my poor turn, to help you see it too,
As though these leaves could be as rich as those,
That red and gold might glimmer in your eye,
That autumn might unfold again in you,
Feeling with me what falling leaves disclose.

On Prebend's Bridge, Durham

I linger on this bridge above the flow
And idle stir, the swirl of the slow Wear,
Whose purling turns and gentle fallings call
Some inner spring to stir and rise in me.
The morning light lies richly on each arch
And signs its bright reflections on their stone,
Telling me more than I can see or know.
I am a passing eddy in the flow
And force of centuries that raised this hill,
That shaped this sheer peninsula and let
The Wear's close curve enclose the city's crown.
Above me on that crown I sense the pull
And presence, hidden deep within their shrines,
Of saints through whom the primal spring still flows:
Bede in the west and Cuthbert in the east,
A field of force in flux between two poles.
Perhaps the great cathedral is a bridge
Above the hush and hum of their exchange,
Pushing and pulling through the pulse of things.

And now a bell is calling me to climb
And take my place with others where the choir
Unbinds a waiting *Sanctus* from its chords
And joins our voices, in rich Latin words,
With all the company of heaven and earth,
And with these two, between whose hearts we sing.

Cuthbert's Gospel

I stand in awe before this little book,
The gospel that lay close on Cuthbert's breast,
Its Coptic binding and red leather-work
As sound and beautiful as when they placed
This treasure with the treasure they loved best
And set them sailing through the centuries
Until these coffined riches came to rest
In front of me as open mysteries.

But as I look I seem to hear him speak:
'This book is precious but don't waste your breath
On bindings and half uncials[1] and the like,
Breathe in the promise of a better birth,
Tolle et Lege,[2] try and find it true,
The bound Word waits to be made flesh in you.'

---

1 Uncial is a clear and beautiful form of script used in books and manuscripts between the fourth and eighth centuries.

2 Take and read. These are the words St Augustine heard miraculously and which prompted him to open up a Bible and read, during the course of his conversion (*Confessions*, Bk 8, Ch. 12).

Bible Study

Open the text again to every question:
Its lexicon of possibility,
Its origin and form and *Sitz im Leben*,[1]
Its deep resistance and its clarity.
Untwist the thread of prejudice that binds you,
Pattern the fragments and reshape the shards,
Be lost in reading till the reading finds you,
Discern the Word that underpins the words.
Begin at the beginning, make an end
Of all your old evasions, make a start
Counting the countless stars, the grains of sand,
And find in them the fragments of your heart.
Open the text again, for it is true,
The Book you open always opens you.

---

1 Setting in life, or life setting. This term is often used by form critics seeking to determine the original context of a fragment of Scripture.

A Sonnet for the Unseen

So much goes unseen and stays unsaid,
So much that carers keep within their hearts;
The children who get parents out of bed,
Already tired before their school day starts,
The neighbours who keep giving up their time,
To add a daily round of extra care,
Veronicas who cleanse the sweat and grime,
And those whose gift is simply being there,
The patient partners lifting up a cross
To bear the burden their belovèd bears,
Who ease each other through the pain and loss
And feel that no one sees, and no one cares.
But there is One to hear, to feel, to see
And he will say, 'Ye did it unto me.'

Four Saints

I St Valentine

Why should this martyr be the saint of love?
A quiet man of unexpected courage,
A celibate who celebrated marriage,
An ageing priest with nothing left to prove,
He loved the young and made their plight his cause.
He called for fruitfulness, not waste in wars,
He found a sure foundation, stood his ground,
And gave his life to guard the love he'd found.

Why should this martyr be our Valentine?
Perhaps because he kept his covenant,
Perhaps because, with prayer still resonant,
He pledged the Bridegroom's love in holy wine,
Perhaps because the echo of his name
Can kindle love again to living flame.

II St Patrick

Six years a slave, and then you slipped the yoke,
Till Christ recalled you, through your captors' cries!
Patrick, you had the courage to turn back,
With open love to your old enemies,
Serving them now in Christ, not in their chains,
Bringing the freedom he gave you to share.
You heard the voice of Ireland. In your veins
Her passion and compassion burned like fire.

Now you rejoice amidst the three-in-one,
Refreshed in love and blessing all you knew,
Look back on us and bless us, Ireland's son,
And plant the staff of prayer in all we do:
A gospel seed that flowers in belief,
A greening glory, coming into leaf.

III St John of the Cross

Deep in the dark your brothers locked you up
But not so deep as your dear Love could dive.
There at the end of colour, sense and shape,
The dark dead end that tells us we're alive,
You sang aloud and found your absent lover.
As light's true end comes with the end of light,
In the rich midnight came the lovely other,
You saw him plain although it was the night.

And now you call us all to hear that fountain,
Singing and playing well before the dawn,
The sun is still below this shadowed mountain,
We wait in darkness for him to be born.
Before he rises, light-winged with the lark,
We'll meet with our belovèd in the dark.

IV Nicholas Ferrar

In memoriam Susan Gray

You died the hour you used to rise for prayer.
In that rich hush beneath all other sounds,
You rose at one and took the midnight air,
Rising and falling on the wings and rounds
Of psalms and silence. The December stars
Shine clear above the Giddings, promised light
For those who dwell in darkness. Morning stirs
The household. From the folds of sleep, the late
Risers wake to find you gone, and pray
Through pain and grief to bless your journey home;
Those last glad steps in the right good old way
Up to the door where Love will bid you welcome.
Love draws us too, towards your grave and haven,
We greet you at the very gate of heaven.

Launde Abbey on St Lucy's Day

St Lucy's day is brief and bright with frost,
In round-cupped dew ponds shallow waters freeze,
Delicate fronds and rushes are held fast,
The low sun brings a contrast to the trees
Whose naked branches, dark against the skies
And fringed with glory by the light behind,
In patterns too severe for tired eyes,
Burn their bright image on the weary mind.
St Lucy's sun still bathes these abbey walls
And in her garden rose-stalks stark and bare
Shine in a frosty light that yet recalls
The glory of the summer roses there.
Though winter night will soon surround us here,
Another Advent comes, Dayspring is near.

In Praise of Decay

So much is deadly in the shiny new,
Persistent plastic choking out our life,
The landfill of each ego's empty stuff,
Where poison and possession still accrue.
So praise him in the old and mouldering:
In pale gold leaf-fall losing shape and edge,
In mottled compost rustling and rich,
From which the stuff of life is still unfolding.

Change and decay is what our plastic needs
To break the bleak persistence of our waste.
Pray that we learn the lost arts of our past,
The arts of letting go and sowing seeds,
That secrets of the lowly and the least
Might save us from the dreadful things that last.

Because We Hunkered Down

These bleak and freezing seasons may mean grace
When they are memory. In time to come
When we speak truth, then they will have their place,
Telling the story of our journey home,
Through dark December and stark January
With all its disappointments, through the murk
And dreariness of frozen February,
When even breathing seemed unwelcome work.

Because through all of these we held together,
Because we shunned the impulse to let go,
Because we hunkered down through our dark weather,
And trusted to the soil beneath the snow,
Slowly, slowly, turning a cold key,
Spring will unlock our hearts and set us free.

For Luci Shaw

Luci I love the gift you have for *green*:
Green fingers in your garden, a green art
In writing too, a feel for life and growth,
Kindly encouragement and yet a keen
Eye for the form, for what needs weeding out
To give a poem room to breathe and grow.
I sense your patience when that growth is slow,
Knowing that slow growth bears a fuller fruit.
I love your eye for detail too, the rich
Particularity of earthy things,
The way you strike the right note till it sings,
And all you have withheld is within reach;
The poem opens for us, and makes room
For fleeting apprehensions to come home.

A Lament for Lost Words

(On learning that certain words had been 'culled' from the
Oxford Junior Dictionary)

To graceful names and lovely woods farewell,
To *Acorn, adder, ash*, to *beech* and *bluebell*.
Farewell, old friends, I name you in my sonnet:
Buttercup, catkin, conker, cowslip, cygnet.
Farewell, your fields are brick, our books are barren;
No *dandelion* or *fern, hazel* or *heron.*
We'll go no more alone, no more together,
The mountain *thyme* is gone and gone the *heather,*
The clinging *ivy*'s gone and soon to go
'The *kingfisher*'s blue bolt', the *mistletoe,*
Nectar, newt and *otter, pasture, willow,*
To their last rites my muse comes footing slow.
We'll hear no more the heaven-scaling *lark,*
We'll all go down together in the dark.

Hospitality

I turn a certain key within its wards,
Unlock my doors and set them open wide
To entertain a company of words.
Whilst some come early and with eager stride,
Others must be enticed and coaxed a little;
The shy and rare, unused to company,
Who'll need some time to feel at home and settle.
I bid them welcome all. I make them free
Of all that's mine, and they are good to me.
I set them in the order they like best
And listen for their wisdom, try to learn
As each unfolds the other's mystery,
And though we know each word is my free guest,
They sometimes leave a poem in return.

In the Wilderness

I Abraham and Sarah at Mamre

They practise hospitality; their hearts
Have opened like a secret source, free-flowing
Only as they take another's part.
Stopped in themselves, and in their own unknowing,
But unlocked by these strangers in their need,
They breathe again, and courtesy, set free,
Begets the unexpected; generosity
Begetting generation, as the seed
Of promise springs and laughs in Sarah's womb.

Made whole by their own hospitality,
And like the rooted oak whose shade makes room
For this refreshing genesis at Mamre,
One couple, bringing comfort to their guests,
Becomes our wellspring in the wilderness.

II Jacob Wrestles with the Angel

I dare not face my brother in the morning,
I dare not look upon the things I've done,
Dare not ignore a nightmare's dreadful warning,
Dare not endure the rising of the sun.
My family, my goods, are sent before me,
I cannot sleep on this strange river shore,
I have betrayed the son of one who bore me,
And my own soul rejects me to the core.

But in the desert darkness one has found me,
Embracing me, he will not let me go,
Nor will I let him go, whose arms surround me,
Until he tells me all I need to know,
And blesses me where daybreak stakes its claim,
With love that wounds and heals; and with his name.

III Paul Blinded Being Led into Damascus

He cannot see the crescent moon, but feels
This night's wide wilderness. He is afraid,
And holds the hand of one he used to lead.
Through folds and shadows where the moonlight falls
He holds his counsel and still holds the road
As it winds northward. Rounding a last bend,
Paul senses each slight change in scent and sound;
A gradual Damascus just ahead,
Whose pre-dawn hush is filling him with dread,
For what awaits him there is his true end.

Slowly from Ananias he will learn
To touch the body and to break the bread,
And, as the scales fall from his eyes, discern
How Love himself has risen from the dead.

IV Abba Moses the Black

You were yourself what everybody fears:
Sickening terror in the wilderness,
Roadblocks and robbery, as hatred stares
From the eyes of a cold killer, practised, pitiless.
And then you met your match: outdone, undone
By Christ, whose wounds pierced deeper yet than yours.
He came to you in agony, alone,
To touch and parse a gospel in your scars,
And turn you to what everybody needs:
All-understanding, all-forgiving grace,
A radical humility that bears and feeds
The needy, lets them blossom in the place
Where love has planted them. Your martyr's blood
Still seeds and feeds and nurtures us for good.

V Christ Among the Refugees

That fearful road of weariness and want,
Through unforgiving heat and hate, ends here;
We narrow sand-blown eyes to scan this scant
And tented city outside Syria.
He fled with us when everything was wrecked,
As *Nazarene* was blazoned on our door,
Walked with the damaged and the derelict
To where these tents are ranked and massed, foursquare
Against the desert, with a different blazon;
We trace the letters: *UNHCR*,
As dark smoke looms behind a cruel horizon.
Christ stands with us and withstands, where we are,
His high commission, as a refugee;
To pitch his tent in our humanity.

The Naming of Jesus

Luke 2.21: After eight days had passed, it was time to circumcise the child, and he was called Jesus, the name given by the angel before he was conceived in the womb.

I name you now, from whom all names derive
Who uttered forth the name of everything,
And in that naming made the world alive,
Sprung from the breath and essence of your being.
The very Word that gave us words to speak,
You drank in language with your mother's milk
And learned through touch before you learned to talk.
You wove our week-day world, and still one week
Within that world, you took your saving name,
A given name, the gift of that good angel,
Whose gospel breathes in good news for us all.
We call your name that we might hear a call
That carries from your cradle to our graves:
Yeshua, Living Jesus, Yahweh Saves.

Parable and Paradox: 50 Sonnets on the Sayings of Jesus

'He that hath ears to hear let him hear'

Matthew 11.15: He that hath ears to hear, let him hear.

How hard to hear the things I think I know,
To peel aside the thin familiar film
That wraps and seals your secret just below:
An undiscovered good, a hidden realm,
A kingdom of reversal, where the poor
Are rich in blessing and the tragic rich
Still struggle, trapped in trappings at the door
They never opened, Life just out of reach ...

Open the door for me and take me there.
Love, take my hand and lead me like the blind,
Unbandage me, unwrap me from my fear,
Open my eyes, my heart, my soul, my mind.
I struggle with these grave clothes, this dark earth,
But you are calling, 'Lazarus, come forth!'

Repent

Matthew 4.17: From that time Jesus began to preach, and to say, Repent: for the kingdom of heaven is at hand.

Repent, repent! What can it mean to me,
But turn around, let go, release, relent,
Unshackle your dark mind and set it free.
Your heart always knew better, so repent!
Repent the cringing and the compromise,
The whole long sorry settlement with sin,
The lowered expectations, the fine lies
That kept the kingdom locked up from within.

Your demons threatened dreadful things: they lied!
Repent, resist their tyranny, withstand
The false advances of the prince of pride.
The King is coming, he is on your side,
Rise with him now, rise up and make a stand.
Repent! The true fulfilment is at hand!

Beatitudes

Matthew 5.3–12: Blessed are the poor in spirit: for theirs is the king-dom of heaven. Blessed are they that mourn: for they will be com-forted. Blessed are the meek: for they shall inherit the earth. Blessed are they which do hunger and thirst after righteousness: for they shall be filled. Blessed are the merciful: for they shall obtain mercy. Blessed are the pure in heart: for they shall see God. Blessed are the peacemakers: for they shall be called the children of God. Blessed are they which are persecuted for righteousness' sake: for theirs is the kingdom of heaven. Blessed are ye, when men shall revile you, and persecute you, and shall say all manner of evil against you falsely for my sake. Rejoice, and be exceeding glad: for great is your reward in heaven: for so persecuted they the prophets which were before you.

I bless you, who have spelt your blessings out,
And set this lovely lantern on a hill
Lightening darkness and dispelling doubt
By lifting for a little while the veil.
For longing is the veil of satisfaction,
And grief the veil of future happiness.
I glimpse beneath the veil of persecution
The coming kingdom's overflowing bliss.

Oh, make me pure of heart and help me see,
Amongst the shadows and amidst the mourning,
The promised Comforter, alive and free,
The kingdom coming and the Son returning,
That even in this pre-dawn dark I might
At once reveal and revel in your light.

As If

Matthew 5.42: Give to him that asketh thee, and from him that would borrow of thee turn not thou away.

The Giver of all gifts asks *me* to give!
The Fountain from which every good thing flows,
The Life who spends himself that all might live,
The Root whence every bud and blossom grows,
Calls me, as if I knew no limitation,
As if I focused all his hidden force,
To be creative with his new creation,
To find my flow in him, my living source,
To live as if I had no fear of losing,
To spend as if I had no need to earn,
To turn my cheek as if it felt no bruising,
To lend as if I needed no return,
As if my debts and sins were all forgiven,
As if I too could body forth his heaven.

Like Unto Leaven

Matthew 13.33: Another parable spake he unto them; The kingdom of heaven is like unto leaven, which a woman took, and hid in three measures of meal, till the whole was leavened.

'The kingdom is like leaven in the grain.'
A woman knows the secret of this word
For she has nursed the rising life within,
The nine-month-hidden miracle of God.
Our Lady took and hid the precious leaven,
A secret ferment working in the dark,
For even there within her inner haven
Our Lord began in us his own good work,
And earth was leavened with the grace of heaven,
That raises us to life, body and soul.
In Bethlehem the staff of life lay hidden,
The only broken thing that makes us whole,
The mystery whereby the world is fed,
For Bethlehem itself means 'House of Bread'.

So Loved the World

John 3.16–17: For God so loved the world, that he gave his only begotten Son, that whosoever believeth in him should not perish, but have everlasting life. For God sent not his Son into the world to condemn the world; but that the world through him might be saved.

The whole round world, in Greek the total *cosmos*,
Is all encompassed in this loving word;
Not just the righteous, right on, and religious
But every one of whom you've ever heard,
And all the throng you don't know or ignore,
For everyone is precious in his sight,
Chosen and cherished, loved, redeemed, before
The circling cosmos ever saw the light.

He set us in the world that we might flourish,
That his belovèd world might live through us.
We chose instead that all of this should perish
And turned his every blessing to a curse.
And now he gives himself, as life and light,
That we might choose in him to set things right.

The Least of All Seeds

Matthew 13.31–32: Another parable put he forth unto them, saying, The kingdom of heaven is like to a grain of mustard seed, which a man took, and sowed in his field: Which indeed is the least of all seeds: but when it is grown, it is the greatest among herbs, and becometh a tree, so that the birds of the air come and lodge in the branches thereof.

Least of all seeds; a singularity,
Complete compression of the infinite,
Still point containing all polarity,
Sown in the field of being by your love.
Simplicity begets the intricate;
A coming cosmos, waiting to explode,
Flings out this whirling world in which we move,
Brings us to birth within our own abode.

So too your kingdom comes: a single seed
Too tiny to be seen, sown in the womb,
And then sown deeper still, to meet our need,
A second sowing in the stone cold tomb.
Till in your spring and growth, alive and free,
You raise us to the branches of your tree.

It's Not Fair!

Mark 7.24–30: [Jesus] entered into an house, and would have no man know it: but he could not be hid. For a certain woman, whose young daughter had an unclean spirit, heard of him, and came and fell at his feet: The woman was a Greek, a Syrophenician by nation; and she besought him that he would cast forth the devil out of her daughter. But Jesus said unto her, Let the children first be filled: for it is not meet to take the children's bread, and to cast it unto the dogs. And she answered and said unto him, Yes, Lord: yet the dogs under the table eat of the children's crumbs. And he said unto her, For this saying go thy way; the devil is gone out of thy daughter. And when she was come to her house, she found the devil gone out, and her daughter laid upon the bed.

It's just not fair – the phrase was on your lips,
It's just not fair I can't do any more.
Exhausted, all your glory in eclipse,
You sought escape but she beat down your door.
Already daunted by the thankless task
Of bringing your own people back to God,
And now the Gentiles come – too much to ask –
So you respond with this exhausted word.

But she comes back in playful raillery,
Takes up and turns and tunes your metaphor,
Teaches you more of who you're meant to be
And so renews your power to give more,
You learn, self-emptied, in humility,
That even crumbs of love can make us free.

Be Opened

Mark 7.31–37: And again, departing from the coasts of Tyre and Sidon, he came unto the sea of Galilee, through the midst of the coasts of Decapolis. And they bring unto him one that was deaf, and had an impediment in his speech; and they beseech him to put his hand upon him. And he took him aside from the multitude, and put his fingers into his ears, and he spit, and touched his tongue; And looking up to heaven, he sighed, and saith unto him, EPHPHATHA, *that is, Be opened. And straightway, his ears were opened, and the string of his tongue was loosed, and he spake plain. And he charged them that they should tell no man: but the more he charged them, so much the more a great deal they published it; And were beyond measure astonished, saying, He hath done all things well: he maketh both the deaf to hear, and the dumb to speak.*

Be opened. Oh, if only we might be!
Speak to a heart that's closed in on itself:
'*Be opened* and the truth will set you free.'
Speak to a world imprisoned in its wealth:
'*Be opened!* Learn to learn from poverty.'
Speak to a church that closes and excludes,
And makes rejection its own litany:
'*Be opened, opened* to the multitudes
For whom I died but whom you have dismissed.
Be opened, opened, opened,' how you sigh
And still we do not hear you. We have missed
Both cry and crisis, we make no reply.
Take us aside, for we are deaf and dumb.
Spit on us, Lord, and touch each tongue-tied tongue.

Whoever Welcomes

Mark 9.36-37: Then he took a little child and put it among them; and taking it in his arms, he said to them, 'Whoever welcomes one such child in my name welcomes me, and whoever welcomes me welcomes not me but the one who sent me.' (NRSV)

Welcome, the word is always on your lips,
Each welcome warms another one inside,
An interleaving of relationships,
An open door where arms are open wide.
First welcome to the child and through the child
A welcome to the Saviour of the world,
And through the Saviour's welcome all are called
Home to the Father's heart. Each call is curled
And nested in another, as you were
Nested and nestled in your mother's womb,
As Mary carried One who carried her,
And we are wrapped in you, deep in the tomb,
Where you turn our rejection into welcome,
And death itself becomes our welcome home.

Get Thee Behind Me, Satan

Mark 8.31–33: And he began to teach them, that the Son of man must suffer many things, and be rejected of the elders, and of the chief priests, and scribes, and be killed, and after three days rise again. And he spake that saying openly. And Peter took him, and began to rebuke him. But when he had turned about and looked on his disciples, he rebuked Peter, saying, Get thee behind me, Satan: for thou savourest not the things that be of God, but the things that be of men.

Get thee behind me, Satan! What is this?
How could you say that to an anxious friend,
Who only wanted all that makes for peace,
Who loved you, and would keep you safe and sound?
But you see past, you choose another path,
For you divine what we don't understand,
And your rebuke, which feels so much like wrath,
Comes from a heart that loves us to the end.

Speak to me too. Where have I set my mind?
How much of it is in some comfort zone,
Content to leave all suffering behind,
Content that you should face it all alone?
Throw Satan out behind me, turn me round,
Teach me to lose with you, till I am found.

The Words of Life

John 6.68: Then Simon Peter answered him, Lord, to whom shall we go? thou hast the words of eternal life.

You have the words of life, where should we go
Except to you, to try and take them in?
We want your words to quicken us, to know
And be transformed by knowledge deep within.
How is it then, these words seem dead in us?
We neither let them go nor let them live,
Their empty echoes always seem to haunt us,
As daily we refuse what they might give.

O Teacher, we need more than just the hearing,
More than these readings we have set apart,
Somehow the two-edged sword we have been fearing
Must pierce at last the well-defended heart.
Unsheathe it now and help us take the pain,
Pierce to the point where we can start again.

A Sword

Matthew 10.34–35: Think not that I am come to send peace on earth: I came not to send peace, but a sword. For I am come to set a man at variance against his father, and the daughter against her mother, and the daughter in law against her mother in law.

Oh, you have come indeed to send a sword,
We feel it in the keening grief that cuts
Through kinship, blood and culture. All we shared
Is sheared away. New faith is met with threats,
Converts are shunned, accused of blasphemy.
You set the sons against their fathers and
The daughters bring their mothers misery,
They know too well it is not peace you send.

How will you make it good? How will they find
The life and happiness they seem to lose?
Heroic witness can seem so unkind,
Will you redeem the ones whom we refuse?
O Prince of Peace, since you have sent the sword
Draw from that sword your all-restoring Word.

Better to Enter Life Maimed

Mark 9.43: And if thy hand offend thee, cut it off: it is better for thee to enter into life maimed, than having two hands to go into hell.

How much we make of 'wellness', 'health' and 'wholeness';
The ideal body, the unblemished form,
How deeply we despise and hide our weakness
And worship all the world thinks strong and firm.
And how each facile photoshopped appearance
Haunts and accuses children as they grow
Until they pine for their own disappearance
And waste away and never tell their woe.

But you have never fallen for this idol,
You 'had no form or beauty', hurt and shamed,
A stumbling block, a mockery, a scandal,
You lived with the rejected and the maimed.
Don't count me with the strong and tanned and thin,
Count me with the maimed, but count me in.

Sell All You Have

Mark 10.21: Then Jesus beholding him loved him, and said unto him, One thing thou lackest: go thy way, sell whatsoever thou hast, and give to the poor, and thou shalt have treasure in heaven: and come, take up the cross, and follow me.

To whom, exactly, are you speaking, Lord?
I take it you're not saying this to me,
But just to this rich man, or to some saint
Like Francis, or to some community,
The Benedictines, maybe, their restraint
Sustains so much. But I can't bear this word!
I bought the deal, the whole consumer thing,
Signed up and filled my life with all this stuff,
And now you come, when I've got everything,
And tell me everything is not enough!
But that one thing I lack, I cannot get.
Sell everything I have? That's far too hard
I can't just sell it all … at least not yet.
To whom, exactly, are you speaking, Lord?

The Mammon of Unrighteousness

Luke 16.9, 13: And I say unto you, Make to yourselves friends of the mammon of unrighteousness; that, when ye fail, they may receive you into everlasting habitations ... No servant can serve two masters: for either he will hate the one, and love the other; or else he will hold to the one, and despise the other. Ye cannot serve God and mammon.

I cannot serve two masters but I can
Be friends with both. In this strange stewardship
You ask me to be generous and win
New friends, as though I had the ownership,
As though you'd bankroll all my leniency,
Encourage me to let your assets go,
And underwrite a generosity
That debtors in this world may never know.

My debts to you are more than I can pay
And now I say to you the very same:
'Quick, take my bill, and wash my debts away
And I will make you welcome in my home,
Then out of all this debt and desperation
You'll call me to a lasting habitation.'

The Good Samaritan

Luke 10.25–37: And, behold, a certain lawyer stood up, and tempted him, saying, Master, what shall I do to inherit eternal life? He said unto them, What is written in the law? how readest thou? And he answering said, Thou shalt love the Lord thy God with all thy heart, and with all thy soul, and with all thy strength, and with all thy mind; and thy neighbour as thyself. And he said unto him, Thou hast answered right: this do, and thou shalt live. But he, willing to justify himself, said unto Jesus, And who is my neighbour? And Jesus answering said, A certain man went down from Jerusalem to Jericho, and fell among thieves, which stripped him of his raiment, and wounded him, and departed, leaving him half dead. And by chance there came down a certain priest that way: and when he saw him, he passed by on the other side. And likewise a Levite, when he was at the place, came and looked on him, and passed by on the other side. But a certain Samaritan, as he journeyed, came where he was: and when he saw him, he had compassion on him. And went to him, and bound up his wounds, pouring in oil and wine, and set him on his own beast, and brought him to an inn, and took care of him. And on the morrow when he departed, he took out two pence, and gave them to the host, and said unto him, Take care of him; and whatsoever thou spendest more, when I come again, I will repay thee. Which now of these three, thinkest thou, was neighbour unto him that fell among the thieves? And he said, He that shewed mercy on him. Then said Jesus unto him, Go, and do thou likewise.

How do we hear again the force of this,
Since 'Good Samaritan' slips off the tongue
As comfortable a phrase as any is,
Worn smooth because we've heard it for so long?
Who is my neighbour? We don't need to ask,
We know that we already know the answer,
We know the duty but we shun the task.
Fear of the other grips us like a pincer:
What if they crossed our path, these refugees?
Who'd meet the cost when needs just multiply?
We fear these questions and our spirits freeze,
It's easier to turn and walk on by.
Cross over to us, whose dark paths are crossed,
Samaritan, whose cross defrays all cost.

Imagine

Luke 6.37: Judge not, and ye shall not be judged: condemn not, and ye shall not be condemned: forgive, and ye shall be forgiven.

Do not judge, and you will not be judged.
Imagine if we took these words to heart,
Unselved ourselves and took another's part,
Silenced the accuser, dropped the grudge ...
Do not condemn, you will not be condemned.
Imagine if we lived our lives from this
And met each other's outcasts face to face,
Imagine if the blood-dimmed tide was stemmed.
Forgive and you yourselves will be forgiven.
What if we walked together on this path,
What if the whole world laid aside its wrath,
And things were done on earth as though in heaven,
As though the heart's dark knots were all undone,
As though this dreamer weren't the only one?

Good Measure

Luke 6.38: Give, and it shall be given unto you: good measure,
pressed down, and shaken together, and running over, shall men give
into your bosom. For with the same measure that ye mete withal it
shall be measured to you again.

More than good measure, measure of all things,
Pleroma[1] overflowing to our need,
Fullness of glory, all that glory brings,
Unguessed-at blessing, springing from each seed,
Even the things within the world you make
Give more than all they have, for they are more
Than all they are. Gifts given for the sake
Of love keep giving; draw us to the core,
Where love and giving come from: the rich source
That wells within the fullness of the world,
The reservoir, the never-spent resource,
Poured out in wounded love, until it spilled
Even from your body on the cross;
The heart's blood of our maker shed for us.

---

1 Fullness, especially the fullness of the divine nature, as for example in
Colossians 2.9.

The Sower

Matthew 13.3–9: And he spake many things unto them in parables, saying, Behold, a sower went forth to sow; And when he sowed, some seeds fell by the way side, and the fowls came and devoured them up: Some fell upon stony places, where they had not much earth: and forthwith they sprung up, because they had no deepness of earth: And when the sun was up, they were scorched; and because they had no root, they withered away. And some fell among thorns; and the thorns sprung up, and choked them: But other fell into good ground, and brought forth fruit, some an hundredfold, some sixty-fold, some thirtyfold. Who hath ears to hear, let him hear.

I love your simple story of the sower
With all its close attention to the soil,
Its movement from the knowledge to the knower,
Its take on the tenacity of toil.

I feel the fall of seed a sower scatters
So equally available to all,
Your story takes me straight to all that matters
Yet understands the reasons why I fall.

Oh deepen me where I am thin and shallow,
Uproot in me the thistle and the thorn,
Keep far from me that swiftly snatching shadow
That seizes on your seed to mock and scorn.

Oh break me open, Jesus, set me free,
Then find and keep your own good ground in me.

By the Sword

Matthew 26.52: Then said Jesus unto him, Put up again thy sword into his place: for all they that take the sword shall perish with the sword.

This word is still suspended like a sword
Above our heads who have refused to hear it,
Too sharp and clear for us, too bright and hard,
Too close to home for anyone to bear it.
Our swords are long since beaten, not to ploughshares
But into guns and tanks and bombs and planes,
And darker weapons still, and hidden fears,
And still the sword of Damocles remains.

What would it take to turn us to your wisdom,
Make us pursue the things that make for peace?
A radical conversion to your kingdom,
A casting out of fear, a deep release
Of trust and hope until that prayer is true:
None other fighting for us, only you.

Five Dialogues on the Two Great Commandments

Luke 10.27: And he answering said, Thou shalt love the Lord thy God with all thy heart, and with all thy soul, and with all thy strength, and with all thy mind; and thy neighbour as thyself.

I With All Your Heart

With all my heart? You know my heart too well,
It's Yeats's rag and bone shop. Will it do
To start my loving in that little hell,
Closed on itself and still excluding you?
Could I not offer you some empty room,
Some small apartment full of light and air,
Some portion of my life, above the gloom,
But not this pit of pride, not this despair.

Only your heart will do. Let me begin,
To break the ground and plant a seed that grows
Up through the closing darkness of your sin
Till your unsightly roots bring forth my rose.
For I have learned to make the broken true
Since my heart too was broken once for you.

II With All Your Soul

With all my soul? I scarcely know my soul.
The age I live in doesn't think it's there,
They cut me up, where you would make me whole,
And think your promise only empty air.
They say I'm hormones, chemical extremes,
Enzymes unwinding blindly, selfish genes,
Just empty gestures and repeated memes.
With all my soul? I don't know what that means.

Before the first life stirred my spirit called you,
I knew you when I wove you in the dark,
I made you more than all the forms that mould you,
And kindled in your depth my hidden spark.
So let them say your soul is empty air,
Love with your soul and you will know it's there.

III With All Your Strength

With all my strength? What little strength I have
Is shadowed by the instruments of death.
I crawl from dawn to dusk towards my grave
As frail and fleeting as my every breath,
And all the strength of broken humankind
Seems only spent on pain and cruelty,
To magnify the malice of the mind
And crush the poor in deeper poverty.

And that is why you need to love with strength,
And offer all that little strength to me,
That you might let me mend it, till at length
We bear the weight together, set you free,
As one who knows how all is borne above,
And meets all malice in the strength of Love.

IV With All Your Mind

With all my mind? With all my open questions?
My restless questing after hidden truth?
With all my science, all my suppositions?
My search for certainty, my lust for proof?
With all my mind? Its logic and obsession,
Its wordless reveries, its language games,
Its reason and its deep imagination,
Its mysteries, its riddles and its dreams?

With all your mind, with every gift I gave you,
For every drop of truth is drawn from me.
Not that your mind itself will ever save you,
But that it lives within my mystery.
Ask and be answered, seek and you will find
I am the life of every loving mind.

V Your Neighbour As Yourself

My neighbour as myself? I cannot learn
To love myself at all. I look away,
The dark glass only shames me and I burn
At what should never see the light of day.

I'll be the judge of that, for in my light
Judgement and healing meet you equally.
The self you loathe is precious in my sight
And I will have you love it into me.
You and your neighbour, both must be made whole.
Her heart's as dark and needy as your own,
So you must love her in her hidden soul,
The very soul she's trying to disown.
Love her as you are loved and you will find
Love is your heart, your soul, your strength, your mind.

Before Abraham Was, I AM

John 8.58: Jesus said unto them, Verily, verily, I say unto you, Before Abraham was, I am.

O pure I AM, the source of everything,
The wellspring of my inner consciousness,
The song within the songs I find to sing,
The bliss of being and the crown of bliss,
You iterate and indwell all the instants
Wherein I wake and wonder that I am,
As every moment of my own existence
Runs over from the fountain of your name.

I turn with Jacob, Isaac, Abraham,
With everyone whom you have called to be,
I turn with all the fallen race of Adam
To hear you calling, calling, 'Come to me'.
With them I come, all weary and oppressed,
And lay my labours at your feet, and rest.

The Seven 'I AM' Sayings

I AM the Bread of Life

John 6.35: And Jesus said unto them, I am the bread of life: he that cometh to me shall never hunger; and he that believeth on me shall never thirst.

Where to get bread? An ever-pressing question
That trembles on the lips of anxious mothers,
Bread for their families, bread for all these others;
A whole world on the margin of exhaustion.
And where that hunger has been satisfied,
Where to get bread? The question still returns;
In our abundance something starves and yearns,
We crave fulfilment, crave and are denied.

And then comes One who speaks into our needs,
Who opens out the secret hopes we cherish,
Whose presence calls our hidden hearts to flourish,
Whose words unfold in us like living seeds:
Come to me, broken, hungry, incomplete,
I am the bread of life, break me and eat.

I AM the Light of the World

John 8.12: Then spake Jesus again unto them, saying, I am the light of the world: he that followeth me shall not walk in darkness, but shall have the light of life.

I see your world in light that shines behind me,
Lit by a sun whose rays I cannot see,
The smallest gleam of light still seems to find me,
Or find the child who's hiding deep inside me.
I see your light reflected in the water,
Or kindled suddenly in someone's eyes,
It shimmers through translucent leaves in summer,
Or spills from silver veins in leaden skies,
It gathers in the candles at our vespers,
It concentrates in tiny drops of dew,
At times it sings for joy, at times it whispers,
But all the time it calls me back to you.
I follow you upstream through this dark night
My saviour, source, and spring, my life and light.

I AM the Door of the Sheepfold

John 10.7: Then said Jesus unto them again, Verily, verily, I say unto you, I am the door of the sheep.

Not one that's gently hinged or deftly hung,
Not like the ones you planed at Joseph's place,
Not like the well-oiled openings that swung
So easily for Pilate's practised pace,
Not like the ones that closed in Mary's face
From house to house in brimming Bethlehem,
Not like the one that no man may assail,
That waits your breaking in Jerusalem.

Not one you made, but one you have become:
Load-bearing, balancing, a weighted beam
To bridge the gap, to bring us within reach
Of your high pasture. Calling us by name,
You lay your body down across the breach,
Yourself the door that opens into home.

I AM the Good Shepherd

John 10.11: I am the good shepherd: the good shepherd giveth his life for the sheep.

When so much shepherding has gone so wrong,
So many pastors hopelessly astray,
The weak so often preyed on by the strong,
So many bruised and broken on the way,
The very name of shepherd seems besmeared,
The fold and flock themselves are torn in half,
The lambs we left to face all we have feared
Are caught between the wasters and the wolf.

Good Shepherd, now your flock has need of you,
One finds the fold and ninety-nine are lost
Out in the darkness and the icy dew,
And no one knows how long this night will last.
Restore us; call us back to you by name,
And by your life laid down, redeem our shame.

I AM the Resurrection

John 11.25: I am the resurrection, and the life: he that believeth in me, though he were dead, yet shall he live.

How can you be the final resurrection?
That resurrection hasn't happened yet.
Our broken world is still bent on destruction,
No sun can rise before that sun has set.
Our faith looks back to father Abraham
And forward to the one who is to come.
How can you speak as though he knew your name?
How can you say: 'Before he was, I am'?

Begin in me and I will read your riddle
And teach you truths my Spirit will defend.
I am the end who meets you in the middle,
The new beginning hidden in the End.
I am the victory, the end of strife
I am the resurrection and the life.

I AM the Way, the Truth and the Life

John 14.6: Jesus saith unto him, I am the way, the truth, and the life:
no man cometh unto the Father, but by me.

Wherever someone knows that they are lost,
And cries for help to find the way back home,
And turns towards their father's house at last,
You are their Way before they know your name.
Wherever someone searches for the truth
And tests each easy answer in its turn,
Stressing the question, pressing to the pith,
You are the Truth they cannot yet discern.
Wherever someone sorrows over death
Yet seems to glimpse the gate beyond the grave,
The living spirit in the dying breath,
You are the Life within the life they love.
You come to us before we ask or pray
Till you become our Life, our Truth, our Way.

I AM the Vine

John 15.5: I am the vine, ye are the branches: He that abideth in me, and I in him, the same bringeth forth much fruit: for without me ye can do nothing.

How might it feel to be part of the vine?
Not just to see the vineyard from afar
Or even pluck the clusters, press the wine,
But to be grafted in, to feel the stir
Of inward sap that rises from our root,
Himself deep-planted in the ground of Love,
To feel a leaf unfold a tender shoot,
As tendrils curled unfurl, as branches give
A little to the swelling of the grape,
In gradual perfection, round and full,
To bear within oneself the joy and hope
Of God's good vintage, till it's ripe and whole.
What might it mean to bide and to abide
In such rich love as makes the poor heart glad?

A Grain of Wheat

*John 12.24: Verily, verily, I say unto you, Except a corn of wheat fall
into the ground and die, it abideth alone: but if it die, it bringeth forth
much fruit.*

Oh let me fall as grain to the good earth
And die away from all dry separation,
Die to my sole self, and find new birth
Within that very death, a dark fruition
Deep in this crowded underground, to learn
The earthy otherness of every other,
To know that nothing is achieved alone
But only where these other fallen gather.

If I bear fruit and break through to bright air,
Then fall upon me with your freeing flail
To shuck this husk and leave me sheer and clear
As heaven-handled Hopkins, that my fall
May be more fruitful and my autumn still
A golden evening where your barns are full.

Let Not Your Hearts Be Troubled

John 14.1–3: Let not your heart be troubled: ye believe in God, believe also in me. In my Father's house are many mansions: if it were not so, I would have told you. I go to prepare a place for you. And if I go and prepare a place for you, I will come again, and receive you unto myself; that where I am, there ye may be also.

Always there comes this parting of the ways,
The best is wrested from us, born away,
No one is with us always, nothing stays,
Night swallows even the most perfect day.
Time makes a tragedy of human love,
We cleave for ever to the one we choose
Only to find 'for ever' in the grave.
We have just time enough to love and lose.

You know too well this trouble in our hearts,
Your heart is troubled for us, feels it too,
You share with us in time that shears and parts
To draw us out of time and into you.
I go that you might come to where I am.
Your word comes home to us and brings us home.

Seven Sonnets on the Lord's Prayer

Matthew 6.9–13: After this manner therefore pray ye: Our Father which art in heaven, Hallowed be thy name. Thy kingdom come, Thy will be done in earth, as it is in heaven. Give us this day our daily bread. And forgive us our debts, as we forgive our debtors. And lead us not into temptation, but deliver us from evil: For thine is the kingdom, and the power, and the glory, for ever. Amen.

Our Father

I heard him call you his beloved son
And saw his Spirit lighten like a dove,
I thought his words must be for you alone,
Knowing myself unworthy of his love.
You pray in close communion with your Father,
So close you say the two of you are one,
I feel myself to be receding further,
Fallen away and outcast and alone.

And so I come and ask you how to pray,
Seeking a distant supplicant's petition,
Only to find you give your words away,
As though I stood with you in your position,
As though your Father were my Father too,
As though I found his 'welcome home' in you.

Hallowed Be Thy Name

There's something in the sound of the word *hallow*;
A haunting sense of everything we've lost
Amidst the trite, the trivial, the shallow,
Where nothing lingers, nothing seems to last.
But *hallowed* summons up our fear and wonder,
And summons us to stand on holy ground.
To sense the mystery that stands just under
Familiar things we'll never understand.

Hallowed be thy name: the name unspoken,
The name from which all other names arise,
The name that heals the sick and binds the broken,
Whose living glory calls the dead to rise.
You make this prayer my rising and my rest,
That I might bless the name by which I'm blessed.

Thy Kingdom Come

Thy kingdom come, thy will be done on earth.
Can we imagine what we're asking for?
When all we know and all we think we're worth
As vanity might vanish, disappear,
Fading before the splendours you reveal:
The beggars crowned with glory, all the meek
Exalted even as the mighty fall,
And everywhere the triumph of the weak.

And we, who have been first, will be the last
And queue for mercy like the refugees
Whom only moments earlier we passed
By on the other side. For now the seas
That separated are no more. The Sun
Is risen like justice, and his will is done.

Daily Bread

Give us this day our daily bread, we pray,
As though it came straight from the hand of God,
As though we held an empty plate each day,
And found it filled, by miracle, with food,
Although we know the ones who plough and sow,
Who pick and plant and package whilst we sleep
With slow, back-breaking labour, row by row,
And send away to others all they reap.

We know that these unseen who meet our needs
Are all themselves the fingers of your hand,
As are the grain, the rain, the air, the land,
And, slighting these, we slight the hand that feeds.
What if we glimpsed you daily in their toil
And found and thanked and served you through them all?

Forgive Us As We Forgive

Forgive as we forgive: the prayer you give us
Comes home so close yet radiates so far.
We set the limits on our own forgiveness,
As generous or grudging as we are.
The wounds we give and take in all our weakness,
The injuries that smoulder, burning slow,
The sins that others visited upon us,
Are ours to hold or utterly let go.

You tell the story of the wretched debtor,
The one forgiven everything he owed,
Who then exacted payment, to the letter,
From one who could not bear the given load.
Oh, lift my given load that I, forgiven,
Might give away forgiveness, free as heaven.

Lead Us Not Into Temptation, But Deliver Us From Evil

Oh, do not bring us to the time of trial,
Deliver us, deliver us from evil.
How is it that your own petitions fail
As evil slams its hammer to the anvil?
For you were brought to trial and not delivered,
You let the prince of darkness do his worst,
The sun shrank from that sight, the whole world shivered,
The fount of blessing let himself be cursed.

How is it? Is it that your dereliction
Makes possible the answer to my prayer?
Am I delivered by your bitter passion,
As you face every evil for me there?
Unanswered answerer, forsaken friend,
Bring me to my beginning through your end.

Thine is the Kingdom, and the Power, and the Glory

The kingdom and the power and the glory,
The very things we all want for ourselves!
We want to be the hero of the story
And leave the others on their dusty shelves.
How subtly we seek to keep the kingdom,
How brutally we hold on to the power,
Our glory always means another's thralldom,
But still we strut and fret our little hour.

What might it mean to let it go for ever,
To die to all that desperate desire,
To give the glory wholly to another,
Throw all we hold into that holy fire?
A wrenching loss and then a sudden freedom
In given glories and a hidden kingdom.

First and Last

Matthew 19.30: *But many that are first shall be last; and the last shall be first.*

The first shall be the last, the last the first.
You make rich havoc of our sense of place,
As every strain of status is reversed.
With one swift look of love, your sacred face
Outfaces us. Disgrace is met with grace,
And blessings fall on those we call accursed.
Strive as they might, the swift don't win the race,
But still the cup is full for those who thirst.

What is this, then, we say to one another,
Planning careers and doling status out,
Ranging ourselves and others on the ladder,
With fanfares for the climber with the clout?
Best drop our trumpets, still our banging drums
And listen for your welcome, when it comes.

World's End

Mark 13.24–29: But in those days, after that tribulation, the sun shall be darkened, and the moon shall not give her light, And the stars of heaven shall fall, and the powers that are in heaven shall be shaken. And then shall they see the Son of man coming in the clouds with great power and glory. And then shall he send his angels, and shall gather together his elect from the four winds, from the uttermost part of the earth to the uttermost part of heaven. Now learn the parable of the fig tree; When her branch is yet tender, and putteth forth leaves, ye know that summer is near: So ye in like manner, when ye shall see these things come to pass, know that it is nigh, even at the doors.

So we begin to contemplate the end,
With shadowed glimpses of apocalypse.
How can we even start to understand?
The heavens shaken, and the vast eclipse
Of everything that we have ever known,
Then, suddenly revealed, the power and glory,
Once veiled in symbols of the lamb and throne,
The all-revealing climax of our story.

About that day, you tell us, no one knows,
But we must wake and watch for you, look up.
Yet hidden in this warning you disclose
A tender yearning, a deep stirring hope,
And bid us, in the visions that you bring,
To see the world's end as a sign of spring.

Refusal

Matthew 25.41: Then shall he say also unto them on the left hand, Depart from me, ye cursed, into everlasting fire, prepared for the devil and his angels.

Jesus, you reveal the Father's heart,
And in your love each promise finds its 'yes',
How could I hear you bid me to depart
Whose every word is bidding me to bliss?
O you who dared descend and harrow hell,
Who spared no pain if you might find me there,
You have not come to curse and wish me ill
Or heap your condemnation on despair.

Any refusal must begin in me,
Mine is the voice I hear that says 'depart',
For I have cursed you in your poverty
And closed to you the heaven of my heart.
Undo my blind refusal, help me see
And welcome you in those you send to me.

Father, Forgive

Luke 23.34: Then said Jesus, Father, forgive them; for they know not what they do.

Father, forgive, and so forgiveness flows;
Flows from the very wound our hatred makes,
Flows through the taunts, the curses and the blows,
Flows through our wasted world, a healing spring,
Welling and cleansing, washing all the marks
Away, the scores and scars of every wrong.

Forgiveness flows to where we need it most:
Right in the pit and smithy of our sin,
Just where the dreadful nails are driven in,
Just where our woundedness has done its worst.
We know your cry of pain should be a curse,
Yet turn to you and find we have been blessed.
We know not what we do, but heaven knows
For every sin on earth, forgiveness flows.

Emmaus 1

Luke 24.17: And he said unto them, What manner of communications are these that ye have one to another, as ye walk, and are sad?

And do you ask what I am speaking of
Although you know the whole tale of my heart;
Its longing and its loss, its hopeless love?
You walk beside me now and take my part
As though a stranger, one who doesn't know
The pit of disappointment, the despair,
The jolts and shudders of my letting go,
My aching for the one who isn't there.

And yet you know my darkness from within,
My cry of dereliction is your own,
You bore the isolation of my sin
Alone, that I need never be alone.
Now you reveal the meaning of my story
That I, who burn with shame, might blaze with glory.

Emmaus 2

Luke 24.25–26: Then he said unto them, O fools, and slow of heart to believe all that the prophets have spoken: Ought not Christ to have suffered these things, and to enter into his glory?

We thought that everything was lost and gone,
Disaster on disaster overtook us
The night we left our Jesus all alone
And we were scattered, and our faith forsook us.
But oh, that foul Friday proved far worse,
For we had hoped that he had been the one,
Till crucifixion proved he was a curse,
And on the cross our hopes were all undone.

O foolish, foolish heart, why do you grieve?
Here is good news and comfort to your soul:
Open your mind to Scripture and believe
He bore the curse for you to make you whole.
The living God was numbered with the dead
That he might bring you Life in broken bread.

I Will Be With You

Matthew 28.20: And lo, I am with you alway, even unto the end of the world.

Your final words fulfil your ancient name,
A promise hidden in *Emmanuel,*
A promise that can never fade or fail:
I will be with you till the end of time;
I will be with you when you scale the height,
And with you when you fall to earth again,
With you when you flourish in the light,
And with you through the shadow and the pain.
Our God with us, you leave and yet remain
Risen and hidden with us everywhere;
Hidden and flowing in the wine we share,
Broken and hidden in the growing grain.
Be with us till we know we are forgiven,
Be with us here till we're with you in heaven.

Seven Whole Days

Seven whole days, not one in seven,
I will praise thee.
In my heart, though not in heaven,
I can raise thee.
                          George Herbert

I

Let there be light as I begin this day,
To draw me from the darkness and the night,
To bless my flesh, to clear and show my way,
Let there be light.

Strong in the depth and shining from the height,
Evening and morning's interplay,
Blessing and enabling my sight.

Lighten my soul and teach me how to pray,
Lighten my mind and teach me wrong from right,
In all I do and think and see and say
Let there be light.

II

The firmament, the vast curve of the sky,
The breath and weave of every element,
Unending blue, wherein we long to fly,
The firmament.

Your love has pitched the heavens like a tent
And delved the depth where hidden treasures lie,
From whose rich womb our life has its ascent.

Out of those depths I hear my spirit cry,
As height and depth give praise with one assent
To that great form that orders low and high;
The firmament.

III

The earth will yield her still-unfolding seed,
And barley sheaves grow golden in the field,
The vineyard and the fruit trees, all we need
The earth will yield.

A soft wind sends the summer through the weald,
In valley folds the sheep and cattle feed,
The shoreline shines, your wonders are revealed;

The waters are unbound; the ocean freed
To thunder praise, in whose depths are concealed
Your mysteries. Your praise in word and deed
The earth will yield.

IV

Lights in the night, the lucid moon and sun,
The lesser and the greater share your light
And lift my heart to you when day is done,
Lights in the night.

And lonely souls are gladdened by the sight,
For those who dwell in darkness hope is born,
The scattered stars still tingle with delight.

Treading the dance, the seasons in their turn
Salute the lights of heaven in their flight,
In our dark hearts your praises shine and burn;
Lights in the night.

V

With open wings a seagull skims the spray,
Sounding the depth below, a great whale sings,
Your Spirit moves amongst them as they play
With open wings.

Now open me to all your Spirit brings,
Move in me too as I begin to pray,
That love may ripple out in shining rings.

Speak to my soul through all you made this day,
Through all that swims and flies and swoops and swings,
And let your Spirit lift the words I say
With open wings.

VI

You made us new and beautiful today,
Your Spirit softened us like morning dew,
Your image shining from us through the clay,
You made us new.

You woke us and we knew ourselves in you,
We walked together at the close of day,
You trusted us and called us to be true.

When we forsook your love and turned away,
You came and sought us where we hid from you,
And on the cross, in darkness, on this day
You made us new.

VII

Blessing and rest, delight in everything,
Sustained by your strong love and richly blest,
This is the gift you give, the day you bring
Blessing and rest.

This is indeed the 'gladness of the best',
From first lines in the east where linnets sing,
To where the last light lingers in the west.

You lift the cares to which I used to cling,
As you yourself descend to be my guest,
And show me how to find in everything
Blessing and rest.

Biblical Index

Mark

Luke

John

CPSIA information can be obtained
at www.ICGtesting.com
Printed in the USA
FSHW010954221220
77083FS